The Mobile Continent

by Chris Oxlade

Contents

CAMBRIDGE UNIVERSITY PRESS

UCL Institute of Education

The world of mobile phones

Many people have mobile phones. Perhaps they just make phone calls and send messages to their **relatives** and friends. They might use their mobile phones in other ways, too.

What do mobiles phones do?

Modern mobile phones are amazing machines that do many different jobs. People use them for talking to other people, for sending messages, for taking photographs and videos, for listening to music, and for **connecting** to the Internet.

What is a mobile phone?

A mobile phone is an electronic **device**.
The word 'mobile' in 'mobile phone' means that
the phone can be carried around.
It doesn't need to be connected
to other phones with wires.
It uses radio instead.

All mobile phones need a SIM card like this.
The card contains the information the phone
needs to connect to other phones.

Simple mobiles

Simple mobile phones can make phone calls
and send text messages. They also play music
and take photographs.

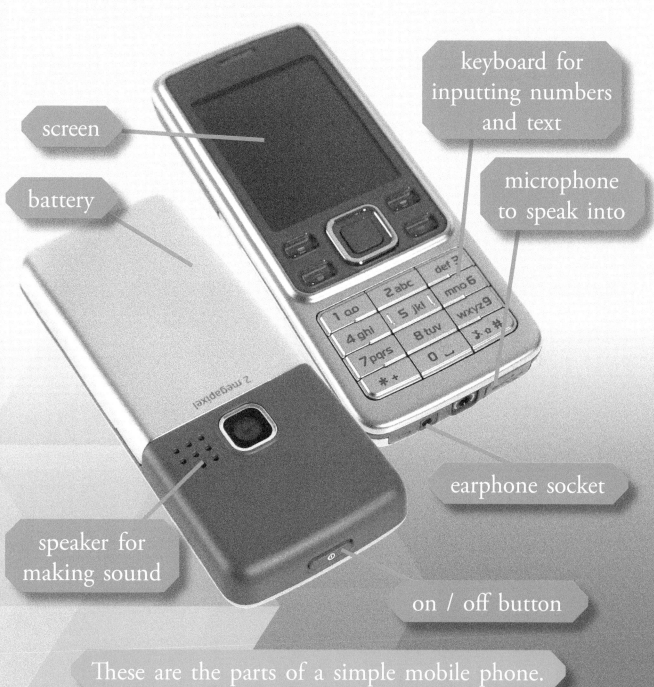

screen

keyboard for
inputting numbers
and text

battery

microphone
to speak into

earphone socket

speaker for
making sound

on / off button

These are the parts of a simple mobile phone.

Smartphones

A smartphone is a mobile phone that is like a mini computer. It can do lots more jobs than a simple mobile phone, but it is more expensive to buy.

Smartphones have a touchscreen. People use their fingers to choose items on the screen and type in numbers and text.

camera

touchscreen

on/off switch

microphone

speaker

home button

These are the parts of a smartphone.

An app is a computer program that works on a smartphone. There are thousands of apps that make smartphones do all sorts of different jobs. The most popular apps are for sending e-mails, for looking at websites, for playing games, and for navigation (finding the way).

Mobile networks

A mobile **network** connects mobile phones to each other. The network also connects mobile phones to **fixed-line telephones**, and connects smartphones to the Internet.

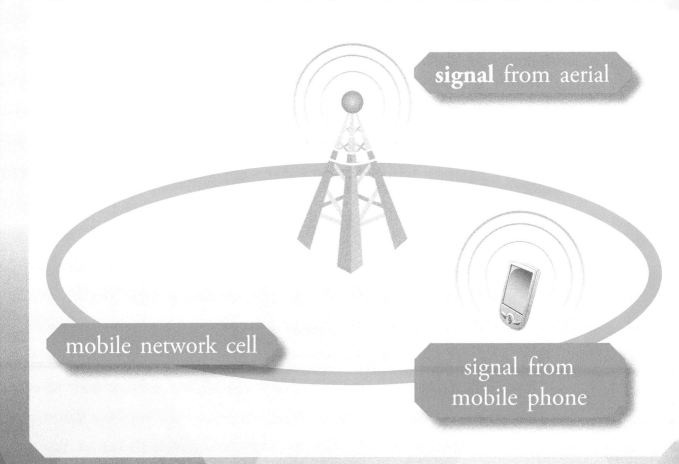

signal from aerial

mobile network cell

signal from mobile phone

Radio **aerials** are part of
a mobile network. They are
found in many places.

When someone talks into
a mobile phone, the sound
of their voice is turned into
invisible radio waves that spread
out from the phone.

The waves are called a signal.
A radio aerial **detects** the signal.
The aerial could be at the top
of a tall tower, or on top of
a high building.

Mobile cells

All the mobile phones in one area are connected to the same aerial by radio signals. The area is called a cell. This is why mobile phones are also often called 'cell' phones.

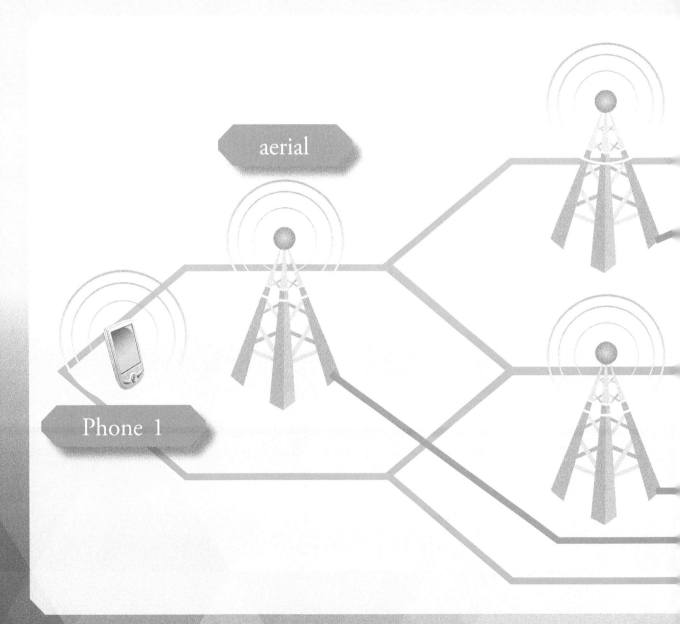

aerial

Phone 1

A mobile phone network is made up of lots of cells, each with its own aerial. The aerials are connected to each other, by radio or by underground cables. A phone in one cell can connect to a phone in another cell.

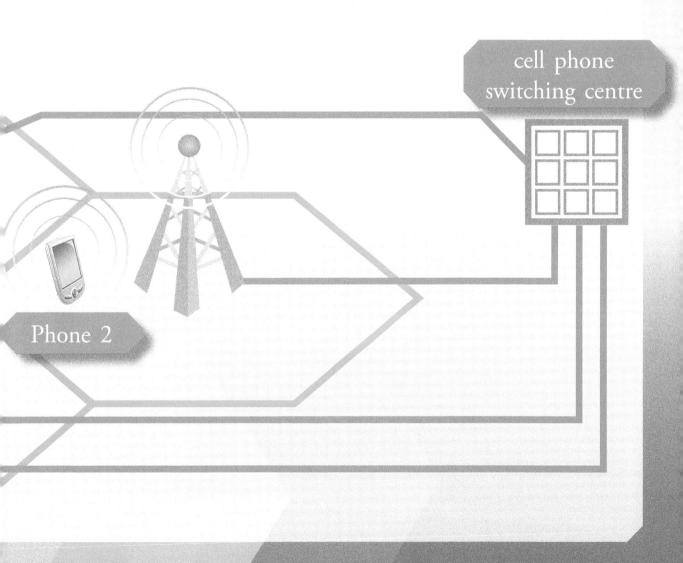

cell phone switching centre

Phone 2

Paying for calls

People pay to make phone calls, send texts and find information from the Internet on a mobile phone. Computers in a mobile phone network measure how long people talk for, how many text messages they send, and how much Internet **data** they use. The computers calculate how much money they spend.

How to add credit

Money, called credit, is put on a mobile phone. When it runs out of money, no more calls can be made. Many people buy credit only when they need it. This is called pay-as-you-go.

Mobile phones in Africa

Before mobile phones were **invented**, all phones were fixed-line phones. Fixed-line phones are connected together by wires.

In many countries around the world most people have fixed-line phones in their homes and offices. But in many African countries there are very few fixed-line phones. This means that a lot of people never had a phone before mobile phones were invented. New mobile phone networks in Africa mean that most people can now have a phone.

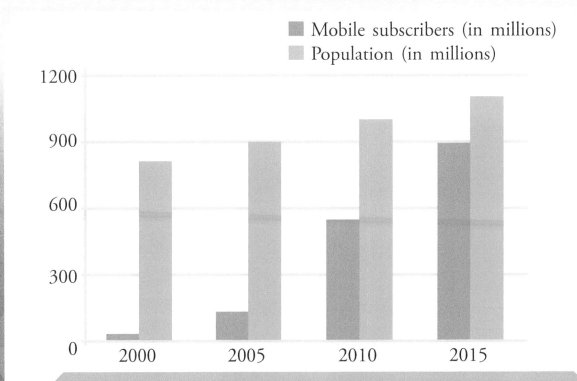

This chart shows how mobile phone **subscriptions** have grown in Africa since the year 2000.

The 'Mobile Continent'

Mobile phones are popular everywhere in the **continent** of Africa. By 2015, more than 600 million Africans owned a mobile phone. That's more than one for every two people who live in Africa.

There are now many more mobile phones in Africa than there are fixed, 'landline' phones. Today, most Africans have never used a fixed-line phone, and a mobile phone is the first sort of phone they ever see. Africa is sometimes known as the 'mobile' continent.

Crossing barriers

Africa is a huge continent. It has high mountain ranges, and vast deserts. There are dense jungles and big rivers. It is hard to connect the network aerials in different places.

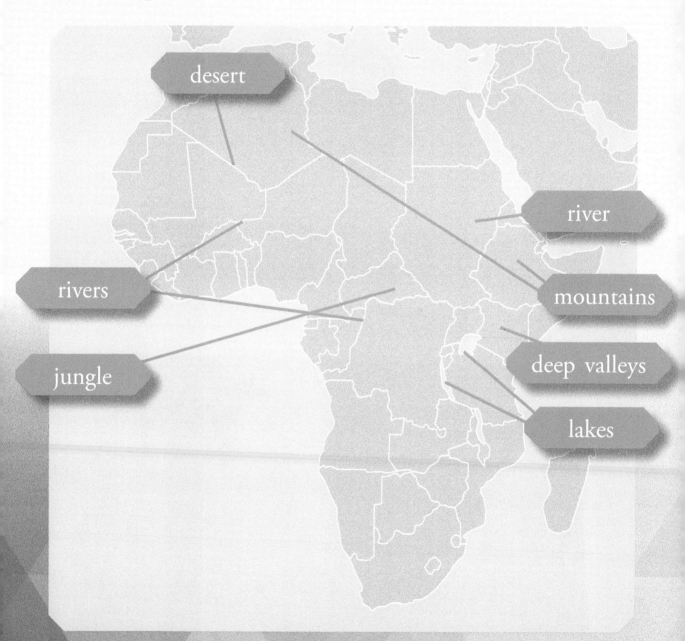

The mobile phone companies have connected countries around Africa's coastline with undersea cables. They have connected **remote** places with **satellites**, radio masts, and optical cables under the ground.

A continent connected

Mobile phones are making big changes.
People in remote areas are connecting up with the rest of the world to talk and send messages. People who have never used a computer are connecting up to the Internet with their smartphones. They can send e-mails, read on-line news, watch videos, and use social media, such as Facebook and Twitter.

In Africa, people have found lots of other ways that mobile phones can help them, such as paying in shops, learning at school, keeping healthy, and growing crops.

Mobile money

In Africa using a mobile phone like a money box is very popular. People put electronic money on mobile phones. Then they use their phones to pay for things in shops, to pay bills, or to send money to relatives or friends.

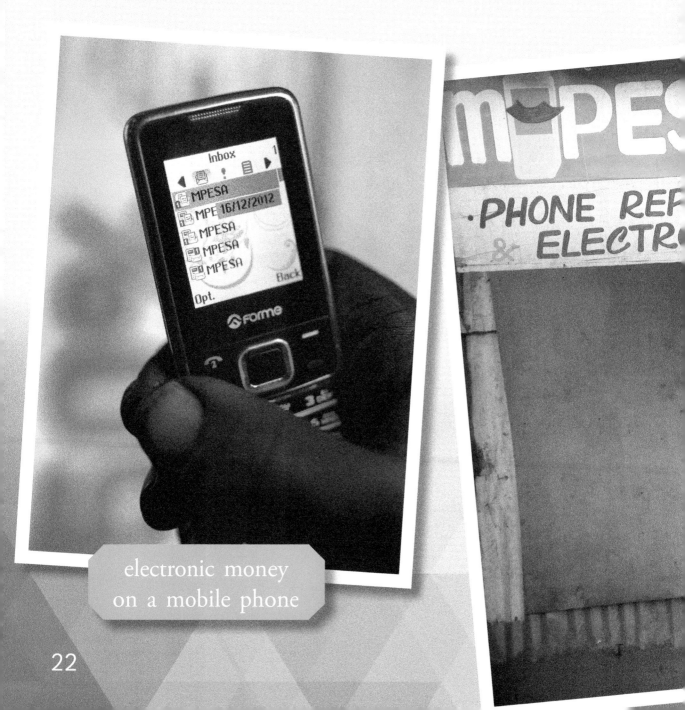

electronic money on a mobile phone

Mobile money is a safe and easy way for people to look after their money if they don't have a bank account. In Kenya, two-thirds of the population use their mobile phones like this.

This man is putting money on to his phone.

Farming and health

African farmers use their mobile phones to get information to help them to grow crops and raise animals. In Ghana, a project sends cocoa farmers text messages with helpful information about growing cocoa beans.

Mobile phones are also helping health workers to help sick people in remote places by giving medical advice over the phone. Doctors also use smartphones to record the names and addresses of their patients and what treatment they have received.

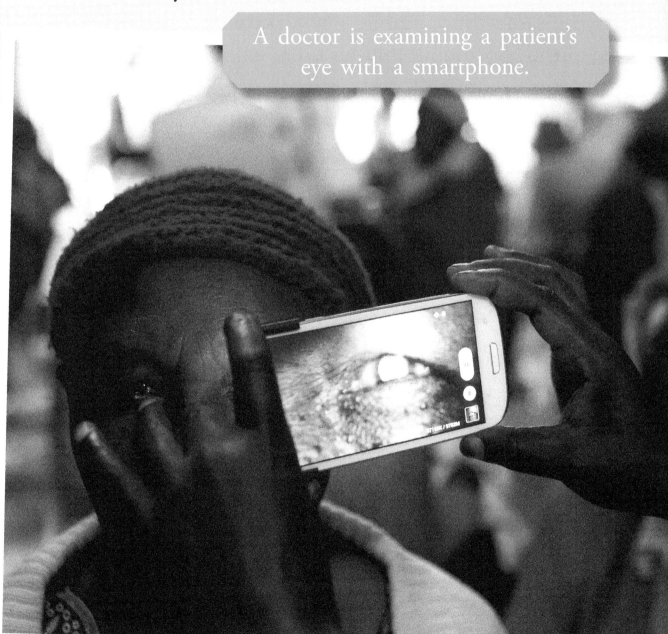

A doctor is examining a patient's eye with a smartphone.

Experts think that by the year 2020 there will be more than a billion mobile phones in Africa. That means nearly all the people will have a phone. At the same time, mobile networks will continue to spread. So mobile phone users will be able to make calls from more and more remote places.

There are lots of mobile phone kiosks where people buy credit for their phones.

In the last twenty years, mobile phones have changed the way that people all over the world **communicate** with each other. Mobile phones have made a huge difference to Africans. They allow people across the whole continent to talk to each other and to the rest of the world. Africa really has become the world's 'mobile continent'!

Did you know?

The first mobile phones were invented about 40 years ago. At first, mobile phones were expensive to buy, and very heavy. Calls were expensive to make, too. Mobile phones started to became popular around the year 2000, because the phones became smaller and cheaper.

Mobile phone history

1970   1975   1980   1985   1

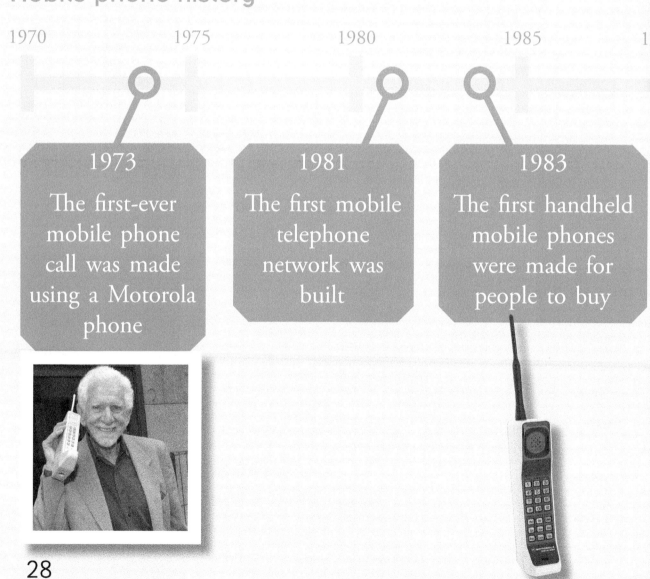

1973

The first-ever mobile phone call was made using a Motorola phone

1981

The first mobile telephone network was built

1983

The first handheld mobile phones were made for people to buy

1990s

Small, lightweight mobile phones were invented

1995   2000   2005   2010

1992

The first text message was sent

2000

The first camera phone was made in Japan

2007

The first Apple iPhone was built

29

Glossary

aerials	metal that is used for receiving signals
communicate	share information with others
connecting	joining two or more things or places together
continent	one of the seven main areas of land on Earth
data	information that is used by a computer or phone
detects	notice something
device	piece of equipment
fixed-line telephone	traditional telephone that uses cables
invented	designed or created
invisible	cannot be seen
network	system or group of connected parts
relatives	members of your family
remote	far away
satellites	pieces of equipment that are in space to send and receive signals
signals	electrical wave that is sent to a radio, television or mobile telephone
subscriptions	amounts of money paid to receive a service

Index

The Mobile Continent ◇ Chris Oxlade

Teaching notes written by Sue Bodman and Glen Franklin

Using this book

Developing reading comprehension

This non-fiction text is predominantly written in the report genre, with elements of explanatory text (as on pages 8 and 10). The book traces the development of the mobile phone and its use in the African continent. The title, as a play on words, will need to be explained to children.

Grammar and sentence structure

- Sentence structures are longer, and include subordinate phrases or clauses, for example: *'It can do lots more jobs than a simple mobile phone, but it is more expensive to buy'* (page 6).
- There is some variation in sentence length to create effect or add emphasis (for example, on page 4: *'It uses radio instead'*).
- Sentences are written as appropriate to a report text using a generic style and present tense verbs.

Word meaning and spelling

- Technical language is used. This is explained by the glossary, supported by captions and labels, and contextualised to establish meaning.

Curriculum links

History – This text will support work on the development of human communication methods around the world.

Science – Carry out experiments related to sound, such as using tin cans and string to convey messages from one child to another.

PSHE – The importance of keeping in touch and the purpose of communication is explored in this text. Children could explore reasons for communicating with others: for help, friendship, providing information, etc. and ways in which they communicate with family and friends.

Learning outcomes

Children can:

- tackle novel, unfamiliar words, monitor their own understanding, searching for help in the text when necessary

- search for and find information in texts, using a range of non-fiction text features
- sustain interest across a longer text, employing comprehension strategies to enable them to return to it after a break.

A guided reading lesson

Book Introduction

Note: This is a longer text requiring reading stamina and could be spread over two guided reading lessons. There are two themes explored: the development and operation of mobile phones and how mobile phones are used in Africa. The guided reading lesson which follows focuses on the first of these themes – pages 2-13.

Give each child a book. Ask them to read the title and blurb quietly to themselves. Say: *This text is called 'The Mobile Continent' What do you think this means?* Establish meaning of the words in the title and how they combine here for a slightly different interpretation. Refer to page 17 where this idea is explained by the author.

Orientation

From their reading of the title and blurb, ask the group to share what they think the text will be about. Discuss children's own knowledge of mobile phones – perhaps their family members have mobile phones. Share your own experiences. Then say: *'Today we are going to read the first part of this book which tells us about how mobile phones were developed. We will come back to this book next time to learn more about how mobile phones are used in Africa.'*

Preparation

Pages 2 and 3: Point out how this introductory page sets the purpose of the book. Note the glossary word *'relatives'* on page 2, and ask the children to demonstrate how to use the glossary. Look at the use of commas to delineate a list of items on page 3. There are several usages of this style of writing throughout the book.

Page 5: Explore the use of labelling. Look at the word *'inputting'* and check children understand what this means. Remind about reading strategies for multi-syllabic words, and pay attention to the morphemic ending /ing/.